# A HEART AFTER
# GOD DEVOTIONAL

## Knowing God in a *Deeper* Way through Key Hebrew & Greek Words

D1617234

## PASTOR BRAD MATTHEW ABLEY, M.Div.

ISBN: 9798636541905

Imprint: Independently published

First, for the honor and glory of our Lord, and second, with great appreciation to my incredible, godly wife, Maureen.

As a partner with me in ministry, she has enabled me for decades now to invest the kind of time necessary to pray, to study God's Word, to research and to write books such as these.

Third, I dedicate this book to you, the reader; my prayer for you is that the Lord use it greatly in your life, to cultivate in you a greater heart after Him!

Lastly, I want to thank my dear friend and my Senior Pastor – Dr. Bobby Hill – for encouraging me to write this devotional. Pastor Bobby, you gave me the confidence for this project!

# CONTENTS

# PREFACE

I went to seminary to do a Master of Arts in Biblical Studies. But about a year into my program, my close friend and fellow student – Danny Gilbert – urged me to do a Master of Divinity.

The only problem with that was that the M.Div. required an entire year of Greek, and an entire year of Hebrew – and I was utterly intimidated at even the thought of learning those languages – much less the intense work I knew it would require!

However, in God's providence, I agreed to pursue the M.Div.; it helped greatly that the Dean of the School of Divinity – Dr. Jerry Horner – awarded me a scholarship which paid the extra two years of tuition!

Never could I have imagined what God had in store for me as a student of His glorious Word – to learn and fall in love with the biblical languages. In addition to that, studying the biblical languages revolutionized my teaching ministry.

Since my graduation from the School of Divinity at Regent University in 1992, it has been my great joy to remain constant in the study of both Hebrew and Greek.

*Thank you*, friend and reader, for *investing* in this book! The spiritual goal of this work is three-fold, and simple: First, it's written to bring God glory; second, it's written to help you to develop a greater heart after God.

The third goal comes in the form of a good request; it's that you would not keep what you learn to yourself, but share it with others. To accomplish these things, we'll pray together each day over what we learn, to immediately apply it to our lives.

In fact, let's do that even now, committing ourselves and this tool to the Lord in prayer. Would you join me now?

> *Our wonderful triune God – Father, Son and Holy Spirit – we hand this book back to You and ask You to be glorified in and through it! Be glorified in our understanding of it, and in us hearing Your Word (not the book!) in faith and in obedience. But use this work to help us to please You, to bear fruit for You and to grow more deeply in You. Use it to increase a deeper heart after God in us. We ask these things in Jesus' name, amen.*

Now, a few words of instruction and explanation are in order; first, I'll be defining, explaining and then helping you to daily *apply* the richness of the various Hebrew and Greek words to your life, from different verses in Scripture.

The Old Testament (OT) was written in Hebrew; the New Testament (NT) was written in Greek. Herein lies a challenge for us; most of us don't speak or understand

Hebrew or Greek!

However, the challenge isn't insurmountable; the role of the biblical teacher is to bring out the meaning of those biblical languages in such a way that the follower of Jesus can understand and apply those words – and thereby grow deeper in the Lord.

Throughout my teaching ministry, I've defined and explained many Hebrew and Greek words to the people I've taught, trusting the work of the Holy Spirit to show His people how they can apply the rich meaning of those words to their lives, to deepen their devotional lives in Him.

After almost 30 years of doing this, it only occurred to me recently to turn this into a book, to try and help more and more of God's people. This is the result of that effort.

I want to thank my dear friend and Senior Pastor, Dr. Bobby Hill, for encouraging me to write a devotional book.

Here's an example of how I'll use this work: I'll explain the most important name for God in the Old Testament – Yahweh – and then show you its use in different verses. Then, we'll make use of what we learn from that name and apply it in prayer.

That will be what we call the *devotional* use of His Word; by speaking it out to Him in prayer, we'll get the importance of that word more deeply into our hearts, we'll enrich our times of prayer with Him, and we'll trust the Holy Spirit through it all to form Jesus in us (Rom. 8:29).

Because we learn through repetition, I'll repeat these words throughout the book, albeit in different contexts and using different verses. Thus, I'll explain and use a Hebrew word on one day, perhaps a Greek word on another, and, for example, return to Yahweh several days later.

*Or*, I may use a particular word two or three days in a row – or more (but with different verses). So, on the days I do repeat a word, please be patient and know that you'll grow deeply as you stay with me in that *strategic* repetition.

Beloved, this book is for *you*; it's for your growth in the Lord, for a deeper relationship with Him through His Word. And, it's designed for you to *participate* and *interact* with it.

In fact, I'll simply say now that if you do participate and interact with what you read, you'll get the most out of it, and you'll find excitement and joy in the Word of God. And, you will grow in Christ greatly!

*I'm praying for you* that God will use this book in your life in greater ways than you can imagine!

Now, let's get started and let's go *deeper* in our relationship with God.

# DAY 1

## *NOAM*: THE "BEAUTY," "PLEASANTNESS," OR "DELIGHTFULNESS" OF THE LORD

*One thing I have asked from the Lord, that I am seeking:*
*That I may dwell in the house of the Lord all the days of my life,*
*To behold the beauty (noam) of the Lord, and to meditate in His*
*temple (Ps. 27:4)*

For the next several days, we're going to dig deeply into Ps. 27:4, in our pursuit of a heart after God -- knowing Him in a *much* deeper way – even in a way that is life-changing. We'll begin with the end of v.4, and each day, work our way back through the verse, to get the most out of it.

The Hebrew word translated "beauty" is our focus today; this word – *noam* -- can also be translated "pleasant," or "delightful." Think of it, beloved – David – the man after God's own heart (Acts 13:22) – knew God as "pleasant," or "delightful!"

And now comes our first, glorious opportunity *and* worthy challenge, but be honest; do you see and relate to God as being pleasant or delightful? Have you ever told Him that He is pleasant, or delightful to be with?

Let's suppose your answer is "no." That's ok; it remains a glorious opportunity for you – and me – because the Holy Spirit *desires* to reveal the LORD to us in this way; it's in His Word!

Let's think of it this way; does our triune God – the Father, the Son, and the Holy Spirit -- desire you to relate to Him with this truth as much as He was pleased that David did? Of course, He does!

How does this all happen? It's through persevering prayer, and the *daily* renewing of our minds with the Word of God (Rom. 12:1-2). These things are what develop a heart after God in us.

I also want to recommend that you develop your understanding of the beauty, the pleasantness, the delightfulness of the LORD by reading carefully and prayerfully through the Parable of the Prodigal Son (Luke 15:11-32).

That is likely the best place in all the Word of God to plainly see God as He truly is – the way David has just described Him in Ps. 27:4.

At this point, the best, and the wisest thing we can do is to pray together; would you join me? **Our Father, You revealed Yourself to David through the Hebrew word** *noam*; from experience, David came to know you as pleasant, as delightful.

We know You're no respecter of persons; You've revealed this in Your Word because You want *all* of Your sons and daughters to know You this way.

So we ask You Holy Spirit to open our eyes, our ears, and our hearts to delight in coming to know our wonderful, triune God – You, the Father and the Son – as truly, perfectly, *infinitely* pleasant and delightful. We ask this in Jesus' name, knowing You delight to grant this request, amen!

# DAY 2

## *NOAM*: THE "BEAUTY," "PLEASANTNESS," OR "DELIGHTFULNESS" OF THE LORD

*One thing I have asked from the Lord, that I am seeking:*
*That I may dwell in the house of the Lord all the days of my life,*
*To behold the beauty of the Lord, and to meditate in His temple (Ps. 27:4)*

In our glorious request, our glorious pursuit, and our glorious challenge to come to know God as "pleasant," or "delightful" (*noam*), we learn a *vital* truth from David: we must be *single-minded* in this most noble quest – to be men and women who do this "one thing."

Mary was a single-minded follower of Jesus; she was a woman who grew deeper in her knowledge of Him, for she understood that "only one thing is necessary," and Jesus commended her that she chose "the good part, which will not be taken away from her" (Luke 10:42-44).

Paul also had that *single-minded* devotion to Jesus (Phil. 3:13-14); we'll focus on that tomorrow. But suffice it to say that neither David, nor Mary, nor Paul lived their lives in solitude as monks; they were busy people -- just like you and I are.

So, we learn from God's Word today that even busy people can still know God in a deeper way, *if* they're willing to dedicate their lives to "this one thing." Again, our *glorious* opportunity, and our *glorious* challenge – and the result – a deeper heart after God.

A person can be retired and have all the time she wants to devote to "this one thing," but if she has the heart of a Martha, she'll miss it.

David was a busy man, with enormous responsibilities and people coming and going with needs, all the time. And yet, he successfully (not perfectly) lived out "this one thing."

My friend, you desire to successfully live out "this one thing," or you wouldn't have invested in this book! How, then, do we go about living "this one thing?"

It must begin in prayer -- as it did for David -- who followed the words "one thing" with "I have asked from the LORD" (Ps. 27:4). In Hebrew, those words are in the present tense, meaning that this was a *lifestyle* request from David.

Let's put that prayer into practice right now (is it a prayer God wants to answer?):

**Our Father, please incline our hearts to live daily for "this**

one thing" – and that is to truly know You in a deeper way -- and to help others to come to know You in a deeper way.

We know from the three examples in Your Word that this is Your desire for us, and that You do want to answer this prayer. Remind us to keep praying it, in Jesus' name, amen.

# DAY 3

## *NOAM*: THE "BEAUTY," "PLEASANTNESS," OR "DELIGHTFULNESS" OF THE LORD

*One thing I have asked from the Lord, that I am seeking:*
*That I may dwell in the house of the Lord all the days of my life,*
*To behold the beauty of the Lord, and to meditate in His temple*
*(Ps. 27:4)*

Please, carefully read the verse above. Although he was an exceedingly flawed man in many ways, God *still* called David "a man after My heart" – and that was in the *New Testament* (Acts 13:22)! Why is that? The remainder of Acts 13:22 tells us: "who will do all My will."

At least one great part of that will of God David sought to carry out was to know Him in a deeper way, and in turn to *help others* to know Him in a deeper way – seen throughout the Psalms David wrote – including Ps. 27.

But as we learned yesterday, David had to make this

desire an *ongoing* prayer: "I have asked from the LORD, that I am *seeking*." And, let us keep in mind what David is seeking: to "behold the beauty (noam: "pleasant," or "delightful") of the LORD."

Most English translations (including the one I primarily use in this book, the New American Standard Bible) translate the Hebrew, "that shall I seek." But the literal tense is better; "I am seeking."

This encourages us in our pursuit of knowing God in a deeper way, because it sets our expectations correctly; this is no temporary matter!

On the contrary, it will require a steadfast heart in this life-long pursuit. However, the biblical testimony is that there is *nothing* more valuable in this life; He is pleasant and delightful!

The apostle Paul was a man of extraordinary accomplishment -- like no other man or woman who has ever lived.

But he would say that his *most* important pursuit in life was Jesus, as we read here, in Phil. 3:13-14: "[O]one thing *I do*: forgetting what *lies* behind and reaching forward to what *lies* ahead, I press on toward the goal for the prize of the upward call of God in Christ Jesus."

**Like David, and like Paul, let us now seek the same thing the best way possible, having read His Word – to pray it in:**

**Father, we come to You now in Jesus' name, earnestly seeking what truly matters to You: by Your Spirit, help us**

to live out "this one thing" – to know You more deeply.

We thank You that we're asking this according to Your will, because it's in Your Word, and You promise us this: "If we ask anything according to Your will, You hear us; and if we know You hear us, we have whatever we ask of You" (1 John 5:14-15).

# DAY 4

## "THE LORD" (*YAHWEH*)

*One thing I have asked from the Lord, that I am seeking:*
*That I may dwell in the house of the Lord all the days of my life,*
*To behold the beauty of the Lord, and to meditate in His temple (Ps.*
*27:4)*

Today will be our final day meditating in Ps. 27:4. Accordingly, we must learn about the most important name for God of all in the Old Testament (OT), and that name is Yahweh, which always appears in the New American Standard Bible as "LORD."

This name for God appears about 6,823 times in the OT – far more than Elohim (God) – which appears a few thousand times. Here's why Yahweh is so important: It refers to Him as *personal*, *active*, and *covenant-keeping*!

This, dear friend, is a major reason David saw Yahweh as pleasant, or delightful (*noam*)! Unlike the pagan deities surrounding Israel – immoral, impersonal and uncaring of their worshipers – Yahweh speaks, loves, blesses, encourages, visits, saves, renews, redeems – and so much more!

Even a light study of the Psalms of David will elicit a thriving, sometimes challenging, rewarding, intense, and deeply personal relationship that he had (and has at this moment in heaven) with Yahweh.

The same relationship is available to you and to me, every day. Let's engage more deeply with our heavenly Father now through prayer:

**Father, we need to know You as You truly are; personal with us, active with us (even when we cannot sense Your activity in our lives), and faithful to keep Your covenant with us.**

**Holy Spirit, we ask You now to daily help us to see and come to know You, the Father and the Son – Yahweh – as intensely personal with me, as active in my life, and as eternally, infinitely, and therefore perfect in keeping covenant with me.**

**We ask this in Jesus' name, amen.**

# DAY 5

## THE DEEP MEANING OF "THE LORD"
## (*YAHWEH*)

*"Then the Lord passed by in front of him and proclaimed, "The Lord, the Lord God, compassionate and gracious, slow to anger, and abounding in lovingkindness and truth" (Ex. 34:6)*

Whenever you see the word "LORD" in your Bibles – that's the Hebrew word *Yahweh* (the verb form is *ehyeh*: "I will be who I will be, or I Am who I Am," Ex. 3:14). Similarly, Yahweh means "He who causes to be what comes into existence."[1]

Yahweh is the name that God chose to use to reveal Himself to Moses and to Israel, in order to help them to understand who He is, at His very core. Instead of keeping His name a secret – an important part of the

1 John Bright, *The Kingdom of God: The Biblical Concept and Its Meaning for the Church* (Nashville: Abingdon Press, 1990), 25, footnote 12.

Egyptian religion – He "expressly communicates it to his worshippers to be used freely" (cf. Ex. 3:13ff.).[2]

First, He is *personal* (unlike the pagan deities around them, who were harsh, unpredictable and distant); second, He is *active* (unlike the pagan deities around them, who were often known to be asleep), and third, He is a *covenant-keeping* God.

By "covenant-keeping," God enters into a relationship with His own to bless them and prosper them, above all the other peoples. His purpose in blessing His people in Egypt was to enable them to be delivered from harsh slavery, and the tyranny of idol worship of the Egyptian pagan deities.

The pagan deities of the nations around the Israelites were interested in the people only insofar as they would serve them as slaves, but these gods promised no loyalty or blessing in return.

In fact, they required the people to sacrifice their first-born children in order to even consider blessing them or their crops. Not so with Yahweh, who seeks relationship with His own, by forgiveness of sins and restoration of the people to Himself!

**Prayer: My wonderful, triune God – Yahweh – thank You for revealing Your vast richness to me; thank You that You're active in my life, that You keep covenant with me, and that You're a prayer-answering, covenant-keeping, miracle working God.**

2 Walther Eichrodt, *Theology of the Old Testament*, vol. one, trans. J.A. Baker (Philadelphia: The Westminster Press, 1961), 207.

I praise and worship You and I'm eternally grateful to You for the truth You continually reveal to me. I offer these words in Jesus' name, amen.

# DAY 6

## THE DEEP MEANING OF "THE LORD"
## (*YAHWEH*)

One of the greatest descriptions in the OT of the nature of Yahweh is in Ps. 23:1: "Yahweh is my Shepherd; I shall not want."

That description from David reinforces Yahweh's name; a shepherd maintained total care and concern for his helpless, highly vulnerable sheep.

Thus, the shepherd was *personal* with the sheep; it's no mistake that Jesus – referring to Himself as the "good Shepherd" (John 10:14), added these words of *relationship*: "I know My own and My own know Me."

To reinforce His personal nature, Jesus adds this later in John 10: "My sheep hear My voice, and I know them, and they follow Me."

Not only is Yahweh personal, He is also active in the life of His own. Returning to Ps. 23, note His activity: "He makes me lie down in green pastures; He leads me beside still waters" (v.2).

There is a third thing Yahweh does for His own; "He restores my soul." Fourth, "He guides me in paths of righteousness."

The sheep inevitably experience danger on their route to green pastures and still waters, by having to travel down deep canyons where it's dark and where predators hide to kill the sheep ("the shadow of death," v.4).

And yet, David is secure, knowing that "You are with me" – Yahweh's fifth activity. Moreover, His "rod and staff, they comfort me" (v.4) – His sixth activity.

Yahweh "prepares a table before me," and He anoints David's head with oil (v.5) – the seventh and eighth activities.

But the ultimate "activity" of all is the promise that Yahweh's goodness and lovingkindness will follow David "all the days of my life" (v.6), leading to the eternal life Yahweh has reserved for him ("and I will dwell in the house of Yahweh forever" (v.6).

Dear friend, hasn't this been an extremely rewarding exercise, to see approximately 11 ways that Yahweh is personal and active in the life of David – and in your life and mine as well?

**Let's pray, accordingly: Yahweh, thank You that You are so personal with me, so loving, so caring, so helpful in every way. Father, please open my eyes, so that I can see and appreciate this more.**

Lord Jesus, You say that I'm Your sheep, and that You enable me to hear Your voice; please help me to hear Your voice speaking to me far better.

And Holy Spirit, I ask You to reveal Your fellowship with me (2 Cor. 13:14) and help me to thank You for it when I realize it. I ask all these things in Your name, Lord Jesus – amen.

# DAY 7

## THE DEEP MEANING OF "THE LORD"
## (*YAHWEH*)

Returning to our study from yesterday in Ps. 23, we see all three aspects of Yahweh's nature in this psalm: we saw yesterday the many ways that He is personal and active with us (unofficially, I counted 11 ways).

However, we didn't have space to discuss Yahweh as "covenant-keeping." But clearly, in every one of the six verses in Ps. 23, His covenantal nature abounds. He does everything for His sheep!

And David recognizes what the Bible teaches throughout – that times of difficulty will arise in our lives – seen in his discussion of "the valley of the shadow of death" and the word "evil."

These metaphors for hardships, persecutions, tests, trials, afflictions and spiritual warfare are all involved in our lives – and God seeks to use them all in a redemptive purpose for us – to make us more like Jesus (Rom. 8:29).

David endured deep pain, struggle and hardship during his lifetime; we can read about it in 1 & 2 Samuel, and especially in most of the psalms he wrote.

Yet despite all these things, David's conclusion is that "Surely goodness and lovingkindness will follow me all the days of my life" (v.6), before he goes to be in the presence of the LORD, face-to-face – forevermore!

Beloved, this is our destiny as well! I have had more than my fair share of heartache, disappointments, physical afflictions and spiritual battles. I know that others have had more of these things.

But they all serve to make me long for heaven – my eternal home which is infinitely superior to my very best days on this earth. And that confidence is all because I know that Yahweh is faithful to keep covenant with me; He is worth trusting!

**Father, how we rejoice in our New Covenant – through the blood of Jesus – and which You, Holy Spirit make real to us.**

**This eternal covenant is secure; it is not based on my performance (I don't earn it), but for what You've done for me, I do want to please You, obey You and bring honor to You.**

**Thank You that You are personal with me; that You are active in my life, and that You keep covenant with me. Please help me to live a life pleasing to You, and**

to keep covenant with You, as You've done with me. I ask this in Jesus' name, amen.

# DAY 8

## PROPITIATION (*HILASTERION*)

*"In this is love, not that we loved God, but that He loved us and sent His Son to be the propitiation for our sins" (1 John 4:10)*

This vitally important theological term really ought to be taught frequently to Christians, and every Christian ought to know its definition by heart.

It's "a sacrifice that bears God's wrath to the end and in so doing changes God's wrath toward us into favor."[3]

It's primarily seen in the NT in Rom. 3:24-25; Heb. 2:17; 1 John 2:2; 4:10, and the idea is certainly in 2 Cor. 5:20-21.

Essentially, it's Jesus' sacrificial, substitutionary, atoning death on the cross in our place; He took the wrath of God that rightfully should have been poured out upon us.

---

3 Wayne Grudem, *Systematic Theology* (Grand Rapids: Zondervan, 1990), 575.

In so doing, our sinless Savior turned that wrath into God's favor upon us – turning us from His enemies to His sons and daughters!

Thus, Jesus' propitiation is meant to give us a perfect sense of security in our relationship with our God; we're saved by grace, we continue by grace, and we're completed by grace – the grace found only in and through Jesus' crucifixion and resurrection for us.

Millard Erickson discloses,

> While the Father's holiness and righteousness and justice required that there be a payment for sin, his love provided it. The propitiation is a fruit of the Father's divine love…Propitiation therefore does not detract from God's love and mercy. It rather shows how great that love is. He could not overlook sin and still be God. But he was willing to go as far as to offer his own Son in order to appease his wrath against sin…. The cross is a fitting symbol of the atonement, for it represents the intersecting of two attributes or facets of God's nature. Here it is that the love of God meets the holiness of God. The holiness requires payment of the penalty, and the love provides that payment.[4]

***Lord Jesus, we thank and praise You for Your propitiation for us; we are humbled and in awe that You did this, in turn, we declare that we owe You our lives! Stir us daily to be utterly devoted***

---

4 Millard J. Erickson, *Christian Theology*, 2nd ed. (Grand Rapids: Baker Academic, 2007), 835

*to You, to delight to obey You, and to delight in our secure position with the Father through the blood You shed on the cross for us. We stand in amazement of You, as You deserve!*

# DAY 9

## "CONFIDENCE," "BOLDNESS," "ASSURANCE" (*PAREHSEEA*)

*"And now, little children, abide in Him, so that when He appears, we may have confidence and not shrink away from Him in shame at His coming" (1 John 2:28)*

The Greek word alternately translated "confidence," "boldness," or "assurance" (Heb. 4:16) is an extremely instructive and significant word for the identity of the believer and his or her relationship with God -- especially in prayer.

It could be translated "fearlessness," especially in the presence of a person of high rank.[5]

---

5 "παρρησίας," in Walter Bauer, William F. Arndt, F. Wilbur Gingrich, and Frederick W. Danker, *A Greek-English Lexicon of the New Testament and Other Early Christian Literature*, 2nd ed. (Chicago: University of Chicago Press, 1979), 630. Hereafter, BAGD.

In addition, it meant "assurance" (cf. 1 John 3:20-21; 5:14-15); it was also used to refer to an openness, or of one who would speak freely or even boldly on a matter.

In Greek society, this word, παρρησία (*parehseea*) was even closely associated with the concept of friendship. Philo used this word regarding a slave who had openness or confidence with his master, from a good conscience.[6]

Thus, the person who has been cleansed from sin and continues in love can have this kind of freedom of speech with his master, who is also the Ruler of the world![7]

In the New Testament, however, the use of παρρησία would more approximate the relationship between a child and father, than a slave and master.[8]

**My Father, I am simply amazed that *You* give me the kind of confidence that You want me to have in relating to You! The kind of boldness, confidence – even fearlessness in Your presence that You speak of – this is *Your* idea – not ours!**

**This tells us of the security we have in You, because of our union with You, Lord Jesus. Truly, we all need to stand much more in awe and wonder of You, Holy Trinity. Would you please do that in us, now – but always?**

---

6 Fritz Rienecker, "παρρησίας," *A Linguistic Key to the Greek New Testament*, ed. Cleon L. Rogers, Jr., (Grand Rapids: Zondervan, 1990), 789.

7 Ibid.

8 David Smith, "παρρησίας," *The Epistles of John*, The Expositor's Greek New Testament, vol. V, ed. W. Robertson Nicoll (Grand Rapids: Eerdmans, 1990), 182.

Revive us in Your ways, and may Your Church live in the freedom of this word and truth, in Jesus' name we ask, amen.

# DAY 10

## "CONFIDENCE," "BOLDNESS," "ASSURANCE" (*PAREHSEEA*)

*"Beloved, if our hearts do not condemn us, we have confidence in God²² and we receive from him whatever we ask, because we keep his commandments and do what pleases him" (1 John 3:21-22)*

Recall from yesterday's teaching that this Greek word can mean "confidence," "boldness," or "assurance" (Heb. 4:16). It could be translated "fearlessness," especially in the presence of a person of high rank.[9]

In Greek society, this word, παρρησία (*parehseea*) was even closely associated with the concept of friendship. Philo used this word regarding a slave who had openness or confidence with his master, from a good conscience.[10]

---

9 "παρρησίας," BAGD, 630.

10 Rienecker, *A Linguistic Key to the Greek New Testament*, 789.

In the New Testament, however, the use of παρρησία would more approximate the relationship between a child and father, than a slave and master.[11]

Consequently, when used of prayer, this is an extremely important word; we all need to be able to approach our prayer-answering, covenant-keeping, miracle-working God this way!

Clearly, beloved, it's God's idea and desire to have His children approach Him in these ways – and we most certainly and always can – because of our union with Jesus and the way He makes for us!

But we can see from 1 John 3:21-22 that unconfessed sin hinders or weakens our confidence. And yet, our Father has made provision for that as well in giving us the gift of repentance and faith in Jesus Christ.

Therefore, let us live soberly, righteously and godly in the present age (Titus 2:12-13). But when we fall into sin, let us quickly and humbly repent of that sin, receive our Lord's forgiveness and declare it.

Having done that, let us then practice that confidence, that speaking freely, that friendship with God, the fearlessness to approach and be in His presence because of our sonship and union with Jesus.

**Father, we do agree with You and declare for ourselves what Your Word says; "there is therefore now no condemnation for those who are in Christ Jesus" (Rom. 8:1). And,**

---

11 Smith, "παρρησίας," *The Epistles of John*, 182.

"therefore, having been justified by faith, we have peace with God through our Lord Jesus Christ" (Rom. 5:1)!

# DAY 11

## "CONFIDENCE," "BOLDNESS," "ASSURANCE" (*PAREHSEEA*)

*"This is the confidence which we have before Him, that, if we ask anything according to His will, He hears us. [15] And if we know that He hears us in whatever we ask, we know that we have the requests which we have asked from Him" (1 John 5:14-15)*

Son or daughter of God our Father, please review the powerful definition of this word from the previous two days of this journal, and then come back to today's entry.

Now, let us *lean in* and in dependence upon the Holy Spirit take this to heart: our heavenly Father *wants His children* to have confidence in Him in prayer!

**Would you say that with me, out loud? Father, thank You that Your Word is clear to me; You want me to have confidence with You in prayer! You want me to speak freely with You; You want me to speak openly with You!**

Loved one, it's when we grow in this confidence, this assurance with our Father that we also grow in prayer. We cannot grow in prayer apart from this confidence, which comes not from ourselves but from and through Jesus Christ.

We hinder, lose, or weaken that confidence by not praying, not being in His Word, not practicing a lifestyle of praise and worship, and by living in unconfessed sin.

It's when we're in His Word and come to know and interpret His Word carefully and accurately that we also come to know His will. John tells us that when we know His will, we can then pray with confidence.

But if you're unsure of His will in a particular situation, part of that assurance or openness we have with Him in prayer is simply to then ask Him for His wisdom, which He assures us will be given to us (cf. James 1:2-5).

But when we know His will, let us therefore thank Him for helping us to know His will and rest in confidence for the answer – no matter how long it takes for the answer – and if the answer comes differently than what we anticipated.

**Father, we rejoice in You; we rejoice in our sonship, in our security, in Your Word, in Your presence, in Your power, in Your providence, in Your love, and in the freedom which comes from You, Lord Jesus – by You Holy Spirit!**

**Today, we give You – our triune God – the praise and adoration You deserve, in Jesus' name, amen.**

# DAY 12

## "LOVINGKINDNESS" (*HESED*)

*"Then the Lord passed by in front of him and proclaimed, "The Lord, the Lord God, compassionate and gracious, slow to anger, and abounding in lovingkindness (hesed) and truth" (Ex. 34:6)*

This rich Hebrew word is variously translated in the Old Testament (OT) as "lovingkindness"; "faithfulness"; "mercy"; "devotion"; "covenant loyalty," "favor" (Dan. 1:9), or "steadfast love."

In the NIV, it is "unfailing love." Clearly, this word is *extremely rich* in meaning!

It may be the greatest self-description by God given to man to understand His nature. In fact, this is how God described Himself and His ways to Moses in Ex. 34:6-7 in a stunning and extraordinary self-disclosure to him.

*Hesed* also describes the way man ought to relate to God, as well as how the people of God ought to relate to one another -- seen preeminently in perhaps the greatest friendship in Scripture – that of David and Jonathan (1 Sam. 20:8, 14-15f.; cf. Gen. 24:49; Ruth 1:8; 3:10; 2 Sam. 16:17; Ps. 141:5; Prov. 19:22; 20:6).

Its importance can be seen in that it appears *248 times*; 127 of those can be found in the Psalms. Although the OT has more writing in volume than the NT, most people would probably think the NT has more references to God's love than the OT.

But in fact, the NT has about half of the references to God's love as the OT does!

Moreover, there are yet more Hebrew words that can be translated "love," which we'll see below.

How would you apply this word each day? How would you apply this word in prayer to the LORD?

**Father, few words in Your entire Word better express who You are, and how You relate to me. You are eternally, infinitely devoted to me; Your steadfast love is beyond comprehension, yet You enable me to continually grow in it.**

**You are *perfectly* loyal to me; You *never, ever* fail! You're faithful to me, and I'm *deeply* grateful to You for Your mercy!**

**Please deepen the stunning truths found in the definition of this word in my heart, and help me to live them out with others, by the enabling power You give me, Holy Spirit.**

May this all give You the praise, honor and glory You deserve, Lord Jesus. I ask this in Your powerful, saving name, amen.

# DAY 13

## "LOVINGKINDNESS" (*HESED*)

*"Surely goodness and lovingkindness (hesed) will follow me all the days of my life, and I will dwell in the house of the Lord forever" (Ps. 23:6)*

The *extremely* rich Hebrew word – *hesed* -- is variously translated in the OT as "lovingkindness"; "faithfulness"; "mercy"; "devotion"; "covenant loyalty," "favor" (Dan. 1:9), or "steadfast love."

This self-identification of Yahweh tells us that He is dependable, trustworthy, and that we can always be sure that this is how He relates to us.

In fact, even in our sin, He still responds to us with His *hesed*, because His forgiveness is rooted in the shed blood of Jesus on the cross for us.

But David says something quite encouraging and instructive to us. Yahweh's *hesed* for us isn't merely "there," in some distant or robotic sense. On the contrary

– it follows us – "all the days" of our lives!

Clearly, our wonderful triune God pursues us – not out of some sentimental, human-type "desperation" (I get tired of hearing Christians say, "God is desperate for you!").

Our triune God doesn't need us, frankly. God is infinitely complete within Himself, and the fellowship within the Godhead – Father, Son and Holy Spirit – is infinite and perfect.

However, His very nature of love (1 John 4:8) – expressed in giving toward us (John 3:16) – is always in operation toward His own sons and daughters. He loves us truly, joyfully, and with His covenantal love – which is His unconditional, devoted love.

His *hesed* toward us is the expression of His nature. When we know it and experience it and thank Him for His *hesed*, we enjoy deep fellowship with Him. That brings Him glory.

**Father, I thank You again that You are eternally, infinitely devoted to me; Your steadfast love is beyond comprehension, yet You enable me to continually grow in it.**

**You are *perfectly* loyal to me; You *never, ever* fail! You're faithful to me, and I'm *deeply* grateful to You for Your mercy!**

**Please deepen the stunning truths found in the definition of this word in my heart, and help me to live them out with others, by the enabling power You give me, Holy Spirit.**

May this all give You the praise, honor and glory You deserve, Lord Jesus. I ask this in Your powerful, saving name, amen.

# DAY 14

## HUMILITY (*PRAUTES*)

*"Come to Me, all who are weary and heavy-laden, and I will give you rest. Take My yoke upon you and learn from Me, for I am gentle and humble in heart, and you will find rest for your souls. For My yoke is easy, and My burden is light" (Mt. 11:28-30).*

To know our triune God is to know the One who – although He is omnipotent, omniscient and omnipresent – is also at His core, gentle, humble!

That is, He is not proud, arrogant, or egotistical. No wonder pride is an abomination to Him; no wonder He resists the proud – but gives grace to the gentle, the humble (1 Pet. 5:5-7)!

But what does this Greek word translated "gentle" (*prautes*) mean? *Prautes* is the humble and gentle attitude which expresses itself in a patient submissiveness to offense (recall 1 Pet. 2:19-23), free from malice and desire for revenge.

Didn't Jesus express this extraordinary characteristic as He submitted to the Father?

It's also the humility or meekness which is strength under control; it's the fruit of the Spirit which enables the believer to place the will of God before personal rights (cf. Gal. 5:23; James 3:13; Mt. 11:29; 5:5).

To be sure, Jesus lived this way before the Father as well. Therefore, beloved, when you and I seek to relate to and know the Lord Jesus, we ought to have in mind and in heart that He is gentle; He *is* approachable!

Likewise, we've already learned the great Hebrew word, noam (Ps. 27:4), which can be translated "beauty," "pleasant," or "delightful." Let us ask ourselves this question, then; when we think of God, do these descriptions immediately come to mind?

If they do not, why is that the case? And shouldn't we then desire to change that mindset which doesn't see Him as He has revealed Himself to us?

Does He desire us to see Him as gentle, humble, beautiful, pleasant and delightful? How, then, may we know Him accordingly?

The answer is to ask! We can ask with confidence, knowing that these are things He's revealed to us in His Word (cf. 1 John 3:21-22; 5:14-15; Mt. 7:7-11).

**Our Father, we come into agreement with You and Your Word; Lord Jesus, thank You for revealing Yourself to us this way; knowing the truth of Your gentleness and humility, we also thank You that by coming to You so**

freely, we can have what You promise in Your Word (Mt. 11:28-30).

Holy Spirit, we now rely upon You to transform our minds and hearts to see You, our Father, and You, Lord Jesus as You really are. We ask these things in Your name, Lord; amen.

# DAY 15

## TO WAIT PATIENTLY (*QAVAH*)

*I waited patiently for the Lord; and He inclined to me and heard my cry.* [2] *He brought me up out of the pit of destruction, out of the miry clay, and He set my feet upon a rock making my footsteps firm.* [3] *He put a new song in my mouth, a song of praise to our God; many will see and fear and will trust in the Lord (Ps. 40:1-3)*

We all know that waiting on God isn't easy, and it can be especially challenging to our faith when we're praying earnestly and urgently over a matter and the answer that we're seeking from God isn't forthcoming.

But David shows us biblically and from experience that God rewards our patience. The Hebrew word translated "waited patiently" (*Qavah*) means to wait, or to look for expectantly – even with eager expectation (cf. Ps. 25:3, 5; 130:5; Is. 49:23).

This kind of biblical waiting is a waiting with constancy and perseverance.

In addition, it is a "refusal to rush ahead with one's own solution to the problems at hand and a confident expectation that God will solve the problem in his own way and in his own time."[12]

So important is this word and practice that Jesus taught on our need to wait patiently or with perseverance on three occasions (Mt. 7:7-11; Luke 11:5-13; 18:1-8).

In the passage in Luke 18:1-8, Luke begins by telling us that "Jesus told them a parable to show that men must pray at all times, and not quit" (Luke 18:1).

It's likely that in God's providence, you needed this today; you needed the timely encouragement and exhortation because you're in the place of needing to wait on God.

Friend, if that's the case for you, would you pause right now and thank your heavenly Father for His timing in this matter?

**Father, we do thank You that Your timing is always perfect. It's true that we wish You acted on our timetable, but we remind ourselves that You're God and we are not. You know better than we do about every matter.**

**And we confess that part of Your redemptive plan in this matter of prayer is to teach us and to build within us the kind of character which was in Jesus. He waited on You with perseverance, with humility, and with faith.**

---

12 John N. Oswalt, *Isaiah*, The NIV Application Commentary, (Grand Rapids: Zondervan, 2010), loc. 6316, endnote 2. Kindle.

As You're forming Jesus in us, Holy Spirit, please help us to submit to Your timing, Your wisdom, and Your ways. We choose – in Your strength – to be settled, surrendered and submitted to You, in Jesus' name, amen.

# DAY 16

## TO WAIT PATIENTLY (*QAVAH*)

*"Those who hopefully wait for Me will not be put to shame"* (Is. 49:23)

What a promise to God's own that we find above! It's especially important to us if or when we're suffering in some way, due to no fault of our own. That kind of suffering is painful.

Moreover, we can easily slip into the feeling of shame. For example, here's a man or woman who is out of work because someone pushed him out of the job, and for some inexplicable reason, he or she has not been able to find a new job.

That's the kind of pressure that weights deeply upon us, and we can easily feel shame – despite the fact that we're innocent in the matter.

A person that this happens to is one who needs God to

provide another job, who needs His encouragement, who needs His breakthrough. He or she is crying out to Him, and cannot understand why He doesn't act more quickly.

Or, here's a woman whose husband left her for another woman. She was wronged, hurt deeply, and she's suffering deep, emotional pain. She needs God to come through for her to encourage her, heal her, and give her hope.

Waiting upon God in matters like this – when we've served Him faithfully but we're now waiting on His intervention – are exceedingly difficult. But when God delays, He has His perfect reasons.

Eventually, we'll understand those reasons. But in the meantime, let us deeply meditate on verses like Is. 49:23; God's Word will encourage us; His Word will give us hope; it will bring His presence and power, and it will change and transform us into the image of Jesus.

Beloved, as important as the pressing issue is, far more important is our growth and our depth in Him. Allow His Word to do its work, and you'll rejoice in the man or woman you've become, in time.

**Father, we surrender to Your will, Your timing, and Your ways. Help us to be settled, surrendered and submitted to You. Help us to wait joyfully, trust courageously, and obey You immediately, in Jesus' name, amen.**

# DAY 17

## HUMILITY (*PRAUTES*)

*"Blessed are the meek (humble; gentle), for they shall inherit the earth"*
*(Mt. 5:5)*

*Prautes* is the humble and gentle attitude which expresses itself in a patient submissiveness to offense (recall 1 Pet. 2:19-23), free from malice and desire for revenge.

It's also the humility or meekness which is strength under control; it's the fruit of the Spirit which enables the believer to place the will of God before personal rights (cf. Gal. 5:23; James 3:13; Mt. 11:29; 5:5).

Given that it's a fruit of the Spirit, we can be sure that the entirety of our lives must be given over to partnering with Him to see this fruit grow.

Accordingly, we can also be certain that with every challenge, hardship, disappointment, test, trial and affliction, our heavenly Father is at work to develop this fruit in us. May we remind ourselves of this truth during those times, so that we have courage to stand firm and persevere.

Humility doesn't come naturally; it's a character and quality of life which must be so highly valued that our choices consistently prefer humility over pride – all so that we can become more like Jesus.

Significantly, Jesus used this word to describe Himself in Mt. 11:29 – in addition to *Tapeinophrosune* – another Greek word which means humility – but the kind of humility seen in someone who is unassuming.

The glory and the quality of *prautes* is *so* important, *so* vital, that Jesus tells us that *only* the "humble" (*prautes*) will inherit the earth (Mt. 5:5; cf. Ps. 37:7-11, 22, 29, 34; Dan. 7:18, 22, 27, 1 Cor. 6:1-3; Rev. 2:26-27; 3:21; 5:10; 20:1-6)!

To inherit the earth involves the highest level of responsibility, and it's one which demands humility. When the saints of the highest one rule and reign with Jesus, it will be first with humility.

God has already had enough of the arrogant rule of people, who refuse to humble themselves before Him. Not so for His own.

**Let's pray: Father, help us to walk in humility before You and man, every day. You're at work to conform us into the image of Jesus (Rom. 8:29; Col. 3:10); because He could call Himself humble (prautes), we agree with You concerning its importance.**

As we abide in You, Lord Jesus, You tell us we will produce much fruit. Certainly, one major fruit that pleases and honors You and the Father is the fruit of humility, which the Holy Spirit will produce naturally within us.

We thank You that such humility is satisfying, like the best of fruits. Pride is revolting to You; humility is pleasing to You. Let Your kingdom come and Your will be done, on earth as it is in heaven with this fruit in us and in all of Your people. We ask these things in Jesus' name, amen.

# DAY 18

## "ANSWER" (*ANAH*)

*"I was crying to the LORD with my voice, and He answered me from His holy mountain" (Ps. 4:3).*

This Hebrew word translated "answer" can mean to respond to in a *joyful* manner; to *sing* in response to.[13]

Right away, beloved, we glean an extraordinary insight into our God's nature; have you ever considered what He's thinking or feeling when He answers your prayers?

Perhaps subconsciously, you've thought He answers begrudgingly. Or, perhaps you've thought that He's so busy that He merely dispenses the answer to your prayer like a machine, and then He quickly moves along to the next person.

---

13 James Strong, John Kohlenberger and James Swanson, "Answer," in *Strongest Strong's Exhaustive Concordance of the Bible* (Grand Rapids: Zondervan, 2001), 6030, 1548. Hereafter, Strong's.

But this simple word shows us otherwise; when our Father answers our sincere prayers prayed in faith, humility and dependence, He does so *with joy*.

Furthermore, it is possible that He answers us even with a joyful song. Let's think about this; frequently in the Psalms – 150 chapters of prayers and songs – we see the psalmists asking God to answer them.

Given that what they write is a song itself, would it not be reasonable that God could or would sing in reply to one singing to him? We dare not press this consideration too strongly, but we ought to think with faith about it this way, nevertheless.

In addition, *anah* can mean to be responsive; to answer kindly; to be amenable to or docile toward (e.g. Is. 30:19; Hosea 2:17).[14]

When it's used of God, it means to respond to with favor -- based upon His own righteousness, mercy and truth (Ps. 3:4; 4:1; 20:1, 6, 9; 34:4; 69:12-13; 86:1, 7; 91:15; 118:5, 21; 138:3; Is. 30:19; 49:8).[15]

**Our Father, it's time for us to absorb the liberating, deep, profound truths of who You are, expressed to us in how You respond to us in prayer!**

**So right now, we agree with You and we say and**

---

14 Francis Brown, "anah," in *The New Brown, Driver, Briggs, Gesenius Hebrew and English Lexicon* (Peabody, Mass: Hendrickson Publishers, 1979), 772. Hereafter, NBDBG.

15 Ronald B. Allen, "anah," in *The Theological Wordbook of the Old Testament*, vol. 2, ed. R. Laird Harris (Chicago: Moody Press, 1980), 679. Hereafter, TWOT, vol. 2.

rejoice that You answer us joyfully; that at times, You may sing in reply to us. We thank You that when You answer us, You do so kindly, responsively.

Holy Spirit, we ask You to sink these truths deeply into us; help us to absorb them and when we pray to repeat them back to You – our glorious triune God – Father, Son and Holy Spirit!  We ask this in Your name, Lord Jesus; amen.

# DAY 19

## "ANSWER" (*ANAH*)

*"O people in Zion, inhabitant in Jerusalem, you will weep no longer. He will surely be gracious to you at the sound of your cry; when He hears it, He will answer you" (Is. 30:19).*

We saw yesterday the rich meaning of this vital word translated "answer" (anah), but there's yet more rich meaning to discover and apply.

God's response to us may also involve a shout or even a response in song (note the three-fold use of *anah* in Ps. 20:1, 6, 9, and the context of the last two uses of *anah* in the psalm) -- with singing (v.5; cf. Ps. 119:172) -- and/or triumphant rejoicing (vv.6-9).

In addition to the above verses, note also 1 Sam. 7:9; 14:37; 28:6, 15; 1 Kings 12:7; Is. 41:17; 49:8; Jer. 33:3; Hosea 2:14-15, 21-22.

The significance of this word to us is at the very least an

extraordinary insight into the nature of Yahweh and how we ought to really and truly see Him: So delightful, so pleasant, so full of love for us that He sings in response to us!

That is, He doesn't merely answer, but He answers with a song (recall that the Psalms are in fact songs) *with* a song (again, note *anah* in Hosea 2:15). This would make sense: God calls us to sing to Him, and He sings to and over us, in response!

This insight into God's nature is somewhat difficult to absorb for us – at least most of us. The truth is that we can never know this about God, had He not revealed it to us.

So clearly, He *does* want us to know this about Him, and He wants this truth about Him to change and transform how we see Him and relate to Him. The entire thought is incredible.

That said, how can we "absorb" this truth? We do so as we would with any other part of Scripture: we meditate upon it (e.g. Ps. 1:3) and let it renew our minds (Rom. 12:1-2).

I've always found that one of the best ways to absorb the truths of God's Word is to use what He has revealed to me from His Word in the form of prayer.

Thus, for example, I would simply say, **"Father (the greatest name of all for God), thank You that You actually sing Your replies to me, at times! Please help me to "see" this by faith, and even think of this truth as I pray prayers like Eph. 3:16-19, in Jesus' name, amen.**

57

# DAY 20

## LOVE (*AHAVAH/AHAB*)

*"The Lord appeared to him from afar, saying, "I have loved you with an everlasting love; therefore I have drawn you with lovingkindness"*
*(Jer. 31:3).*

When used of Yahweh's love for man (cf. Ps. 146:8; Prov. 3:11-12; Is. 43:4; 48:14; 63:9; Jer. 31:3; Hosea 11:4; Zeph. 3:17), this rich Hebrew word – *ahab* (pronounced *ahav*) -- can mean to "have affection for," and thus, it's a *friendship* love.[16]

But this love is also a covenantal term, and it's connected this way in Deut. 6:5; 7:8, 13; 10:15; 23:5-6. We can even say it is a deeply affectionate love, as well as a loyal love.[17]

16 Robert L. Alden, "*Aheb*," in *The Theological Wordbook of the Old Testament*, vol. 1, ed. R. Laird Harris (Chicago: Moody Press, 1980), 14. Hereafter, TWOT, vol. 1.

17 Douglas Stuart, *Hosea-Jonah*, Word Biblical Commentary, vol. 31 (Waco: Word Books, 1987), 178.

In addition, it was used to refer to a familial love. Apart from *hesed*, which is more of a covenantal love, *ahab* is the primary word used to describe Yahweh's love for man in the OT.

It's used of David's love for Yahweh (e.g. Ps. 5:11d; 31:23; 116:1; 145:20), and he exhorts the reader to "love" (*ahab*) Yahweh (Ps. 31:23). In addition, note Ex. 20:6; Deut. 5:10; 6:5; 7:9.

*Ahab* expressed Yahweh's giving, loyal, noble, unselfish, generous and protective love to His own. Thus, it "indicates complete love which demands all of one's energies."[18]

Clearly, His affectionate, friendship love toward His own – plus the definition in the paragraph above – demonstrates how vastly different He is from the pagan deities.

Moreover, it paves the way for the believer in Jesus to more fully understand the Father's love and heart for His own – a Father who is personal, active and who keeps covenant with His own.

Old Testament Scholar Walther Eichrodt calls God's love for His own "the miracle of free affection."[19]

**Father, Son, and Holy Spirit – how is that You love me**

---

18 Gerhard Wallis, "Ahabh," in *Theological Dictionary of the Old Testament*, vol. 1, ed. G. Johannes Botterwick and Helmer Ringgren, trans. John T. Willis (Grand Rapids: Eerdmans, 1974), 104.

19 Walther Eichrodt, *Theology of the Old Testament*, vol. 1, trans. J.A. Baker (Philadelphia: The Westminster Press, 1961), 256.

like this? You call me Your friend – me – the one who has let You down far too many times! And if that were not enough, this word and Your entire Word show me that You enjoy being with me.

This is overwhelming; I can only respond with gratitude to You – and to share this love I have with You to believer and the unsaved alike. Grant me many more opportunities to do just that, to bring You, my Triune God, the greatest glory and honor due Your name.

# DAY 21

## HUMILITY (*TAPEINO* OR *TAPEINOPHROSUNE*)

*"Come to Me, all who are weary and heavy-laden, and I will give you rest. Take My yoke upon you and learn from Me, for I am gentle and humble in heart, and you will find rest for your souls. For My yoke is easy, and My burden is light" (Mt. 11:28-30).*

We studied the passage above earlier in this book, focusing on the Greek word translated "gentle" (*prautes*).

Now, we define Jesus' second definition of Himself and His nature; the word "humble" is *tapeinophrosune* (pronounced "top ain oph rah sun ay").

This word is used preeminently by Jesus to describe Himself (cf. Mt. 11:29-30), seen even in the way He relates to others (e.g. Mt. 20:28; Mark 10:45; Luke 22:27; cf. Is. 42:1-2).

It refers to one who is modest; to one who behaves in an

unassuming manner, devoid of all haughtiness (e.g. Phil. 2: 3; cf. 1 Pet. 5:5). Again, we see this chiefly through Jesus' life and example (Phil. 2:5-11).

It means to bow down. Accordingly, beloved we're invited yet again to allow the Holy Spirit to transform the way we see our God, so that we can draw closer to Him in prayer and in worship.

Moreover, the result should also stir us to share the gospel with others, conveying to them what they really do not know much of at all – the true nature of God.

In addition, as we meditate on the powerful truth of this Greek word and Jesus' use of it to describe Himself, we must equally be stirred to continually ask the Holy Spirit to develop this same quality in us.

So let's do that now, in prayer; would you join me?

**Our Father, we ask You to help us to embrace this kind of humility and not seek to avoid it.**

**If we've been guilty of trying to promote ourselves, if we've been guilty of thinking of ourselves as more important than others, if we've been guilty of walking over people due to our own selfishness – forgive us and work this deeply in us through Your power, Holy Spirit.**

**And let the ultimate outcome be that we become more like You, Lord Jesus! But help us not to stop there; stir our hearts to live this way before those who know You and those who do not know You – whether they're easy or difficult to love or relate to.**

Grant us open doors and opportunities to speak to the unsaved about Your true nature, Lord Jesus, to lead them to faith in You! We ask this according to Your will, amen.

# DAY 22

## PATIENCE OR STEADFASTNESS (*HUPOMONE*)

*"For whatever was written in earlier times was written for our instruction, so that through perseverance and the encouragement of the Scriptures we might have hope" (Rom. 15:4).*

The Greek word translated "perseverance" that we're about to study (*hupomone*) is *surely* one of *the* most important words in the NT.

The chief reason is due to the depth of its meaning; it describes *how* we're to respond in tests, trials and tribulations. Moreover, this word paints an extraordinary picture of us for who God wants us to become like – Jesus (Rom. 8:29).

I'm always amazed at some of the passages that have *hupomone* as its goal and focus – passages in the NT which are highly important and highly substantive for our faith.

"Hupo" (better, "hypo") is where we get our word "hyper" from. The word "*mone*" comes from *menein*, or, to "remain."

Thus, in a kind of colloquial way of putting it, we can say that *hupomone* has the idea of a "hyper remaining."

Technically, it's a patient endurance. It means to stand up under; to patiently wait in hope. It's never a complaining or despondent endurance.

It's consistent, critical importance can be very much appreciated in the following verses, all of which have so much to do with real depth in the Christian life (cf. Luke 8:15; Rom. 15:4-5; 2 Cor. 1:6; 6:4; 1 Thess. 1:3; 2 Thess. 3:5; Col. 1:11; Heb. 10:36; 12:1-3, 7; James 1:3-4, 12; 5:11).

*Hupomone* is the spirit which can bear all things -- not simply with resignation -- but with blazing hope... because it knows the challenges are leading to a goal of glory.[20]

In fact, in the Greek society of the NT period, it was used of that which came upon a man against his will. In classical Greek, it referred to that quality which enabled a man to die for his god.[21]

Thus, it's through the power of the Holy Spirit in daily cultivating this very special quality that we grow to

---

20 Rienecker, *A Linguistic Key to the Greek New Testament*, 705.

21 Ibid., 451.

remain firm in our faith -- no matter how difficult, or intense our suffering, our disappointment or our trials may be.

**Our Father, You've made it abundantly clear that we're *going* to go through tests, trials and adversity in this life. As we do, please help us to continually keep in mind the reasons for our trials, so that we can develop *hupomone* and bring You glory and honor.**

# DAY 23

## PATIENCE OR STEADFASTNESS
## (*HUPOMONE*)

*"May the Lord direct your hearts into the love of God and into the steadfastness (hupomone) of Christ" (2 Thess. 3:5).*

Commenting on this verse, Leon Morris explains that *hupomone* also refers to "the characteristic of a man who is unswerved from his deliberate purpose and his loyalty to faith and piety by even the greatest trials and sufferings."[22]

Without consistent growth in this glorious, vital quality of Jesus – *hupomone* – I'm painfully aware of how easily I can slip into fleshly ways and complain, or become bitter or sullen because of my circumstances.

---

22 Leon Morris, *The Epistles of Paul to the Thessalonians*, Tyndale New Testament Commentaries (Grand Rapids: Eerdmans, 2000), 143.

I'm writing this now because of many current hardships I'm undergoing – hardships beyond my control. Nevertheless, *how I respond* to those hardships *is* under my control – through the enabling power of the Holy Spirit.

Whether I exercise such self-control and *choose* to move in *hupomone* depends on one thing, frankly; it depends on whether I want *my will* or my heavenly Father's will to be done.

If I seek His will and glory and honor, then I'll choose to be settled, surrendered and submitted to Him. If I seek to be His example to fellow believers and to the unsaved, I'll choose *hupomone* over a complaining, critical, bitter spirit in response to life's challenges.

**Our Father, if we're not careful to guard our hearts every day and also to repent of our sinful ways and attitudes, we'll resent Your daily invitation to become like Jesus. And the result for us will only be misery – for us and for those we live with.**

**We won't bring glory to You; tragically and seriously, we'll bring shame to Your name with the unsaved, and we'll bring damage to the body of Christ – the Church You love.**

**Please help us to daily cultivate humility before You and man, and utter dependence upon You – so that we have the right heart to embrace *hupomone* for all the right reasons – especially to become more like You, Lord Jesus.**

# DAY 24

## PATIENCE OR STEADFASTNESS (*HUPOMONE*)

*"Consider it all joy, my brethren, when you encounter various trials,³ knowing that the testing of your faith produces endurance. ⁴ And let endurance have its perfect result, so that you may be perfect and complete, lacking in nothing" (James 1:2-4)*

Just this morning I asked the Lord for His wisdom as to why I'm undergoing so much hardship – especially physically (I caught malaria on a recent ministry trip to Uganda and I'm still dealing with its effects).

I also asked Him what He wants me to see and understand about this, and many other challenges I'm facing. Almost immediately, I had a strong desire to read the Epistle of James. But I could not make it past James 1:2-5!

I realized right away my need of more *hupomone* (the word translated "endurance," in James 1:3-4). Dear friend, I *want* to become more like Jesus; I *want* to honor our triune God with my life and my character!

There is far too much at stake for my witness to the unsaved and my example to other believers if I do not embrace God's call for me to develop His *hupomone* – always through the aid of the Holy Spirit.

The goal of that *hupomone* – James tells us – is that we become "perfect and complete, lacking in nothing" (James 1:4).

The Greek word translated "perfect" (v.4) comes from the OT idea of maturity, as a right relationship with God, expressed in undivided obedience and an unblemished life.[23]

The Greek word translated "complete" (v.4) refers to the entirety of all the Christian virtues.[24]

But again, both are directly tied to our growth in *hupomone*! Thus, this clearly illustrates how important, how vital to our growth in Christ that *hupomone* is.

**Our Father, we embrace Your gentle, wise, present and eternal work in us; we yield to You and Your providential care! We thank You for revealing to us the reason for our trials; they're given or allowed in our lives to produce Christlikeness, humility and godly character. We desperately need the substance and quality of this word; we desperately need that level**

---

23 James B. Adamson, *The Epistle of James*, The New International Commentary on the New Testament (Grand Rapids: Eerdmans, 1976), 55.

24 Reinecker, *A Linguistic Key to the Greek New Testament*, 721.

of steadfastness in our lives. Help us to understand when we go through trials that You're at work to increase *hupomone* in our lives, for Your glory. We ask these things in Jesus' name, amen.

# DAY 25

## PATIENCE (*MAKRATHUMIA*)

*[S]strengthened with all power, according to His glorious
might, for the attaining of all steadfastness and patience
(makrathumia); joyously giving thanks to the Father, who has qualified
us to share in the inheritance of the saints in Light (Col. 1:11-12)*

This Greek word translated "patience" (*makrathumia*)
is yet another rich word; it can alternatively refer to a
"joyful endurance" (Col. 1:11-12), or a patience that
is "long-suffering" (Gal. 5:22). Fundamentally, it's a
"patient endurance under injuries inflicted by others."[25]

It also refers to the "self-restraint which does not hastily
retaliate a wrong."[26]

This is the blessing of the fruit of the Spirit which is "self-
control" (Gal. 5:22); when we walk this way, we live in

---

25 Rienecker, *A Linguistic Key to the Greek New Testament*, 517.

26 Ibid., 566.

peace, and we impart God's peace to others – instead of living in the strain of strife.

To be sure, we act like God when we move in this self-restraint, this self-control. Believers see it and are motivated toward it; the unsaved see it and witness the life of Jesus in us.

What urgency we must have to grow in this Christ-like quality! May we gladly yield to the Holy Spirit when we see Him at work in us to help us, accordingly.

In addition, in Rom. 2:4, it is "a long holding out of the mind before it gives room to action or passion."[27]

We read there of God's "kindness and tolerance and patience (*makrathumia*)," which are designed to lead us to repentance – instead of the just desert of His wrath issued against us.

We're only hypocrites if we gladly take the *makrathumia* of God, but refuse to then give it toward others!

**Father, please forgive us for not exercising *makrathumia* toward others – the way You exercise this quality toward us! There can be no question that You purposely allow or even send "difficult" people to us for the very purpose of developing that *makrathumia* in us and through us.**

**We humble ourselves now over this matter, and we choose to courageously say, "Lord, we want this characteristic to flourish in us, because it will bring**

---

27 Ibid., 352.

glory and honor to You, it will bless others, and it will enable us to be the kind of witness to the unsaved that You deserve!

# DAY 26

## PATIENCE (*MAKRATHUMIA*)

*"We urge you, brethren, admonish the unruly, encourage the fainthearted, help the weak, be patient with everyone" (1 Thess. 5:14)*

In 1 Thess. 5:14, the word translated to be "patient" indicates one who does "not give way to a short or quick temper toward those who fail, but is patient and considerate of them."[28]

Think of it: are we not like God the Father when we exercise such a quality? Are we not like Jesus our Lord when we exercise this quality? Later, Paul refers to "the steadfastness of Christ" (2 Thess. 3:5).

Is this not what it means to reveal the character of God to each other and to the unsaved when they see us walk in this *makrathumia* at precisely the time they would expect

---

28 Rienecker, *A Linguistic Key to the Greek New Testament*, 602.

PASTOR BRAD MATTHEW ABLEY, M.DIV.

us to move in the opposite direction and blast away at someone?

Truly, the development of *makrathumia* is something each believer needs from the other; it's something the world needs to see in us, and it *always* brings glory to God!

But we make a severe mistake if we think that because everything seems to be fine at the moment, that we don't still need to work with the Holy Spirit to develop this trait!

On the contrary, if we're not diligent in this area – even praying for our growth in *makrathumia* (and in *hupomone*) – the time will come when we deeply regret not heeding the sense of urgency for its development in our lives.

It seems an easy way to understand the difference between these two words is to think of *hupomone* as relating to circumstances, and *makrathumia* relating to patience with people.[29]

**Father, as we prayed yesterday, so we pray now: please forgive us for not exercising *makrathumia* toward others – the way You exercise this quality toward us!**

**There can be no question that You purposely allow or even send "difficult" people to us for the very purpose of developing that *makrathumia* in us and through us.**

---

29 Richard C. Trench, *Synonyms of the New Testament* (Grand Rapids: Eerdmans, 1983), 198.

We humble ourselves now over this matter, and we choose to courageously say, "Lord, we want this characteristic to flourish in us, because it will bring glory and honor to You, it will bless others, and it will enable us to be the kind of witness to the unsaved that You deserve!

# DAY 27

## FATHER (*ABBA*)

*"For you have not received a spirit of slavery leading to fear again, but you have received a spirit of adoption as sons by which we cry out, "Abba! Father!" (Rom. 8:15).*

*Abba* was used directly by Jesus in prayer to His Father (cf. Mark 14:36); it was a common term used of either a child speaking to his or her father, or even an adult addressing his or her father.

It's a familial term – not a formal term. That is, it connotes intimacy and family relation. In using this term, we gain an extraordinary glimpse into the relationship between the Father and the Son.

In turn, it was an extraordinary thing indeed for Jesus to then teach His disciples to address God as their Father (e.g. Mt. 6:9); this was revolutionary in His time; no one would dare pray with such familiarity to the Father.

In fact, there is *not one prayer* in the entire OT where an individual addressed God as Father!

So, for Jesus to introduce this word was a radical departure from the norm for prayer among the Jewish people.

So important was this word that it was a common or ordinary way for Christians to address the Father after Jesus' resurrection and ascension to the Father. Paul uses Abba in writing both to the Romans (Rom. 8:15) and to the Galatians (Gal. 4:6).

In fact, another insight into the vital nature of this term in addressing God the Father can be gleaned from observing the role of the Holy Spirit in enabling the believer to call the Father, Abba.

Why is this? The reason is that in the NT, sonship is one of the highest privileges of all (Rom. 8:15-17; Gal. 4:5-6; Eph. 1:4-6).

However, in order to fully apprehend our sonship, the Holy Spirit seeks to lead us into addressing our Father as Father, or simply, Abba.

It is never wrong to refer to Him as "God" or "Lord," but if that is the only way we refer to Him, we certainly must admit that we're essentially being unbiblical, in the deepest sense of the word.

That is, we're avoiding the biblical riches of our identity in Christ, of our powerful, freeing relationship with our heavenly Father, and of the security in our sonship that Jesus died to give us.

This is very, very deep, but it can only be appreciated by purposing – through reliance on the Holy Spirit – to call God our Father. Truly, the more we practice or enter into this privilege, the more real it will become to us.

# DAY 28

## FATHER (*ABBA*)

*"Because you are sons, God has sent forth the Spirit of His Son into our hearts, crying, 'Abba! Father!'" (Gal. 4:6)*

I understand that many believers have had terrible fathers, absent fathers, and tragically – abusive fathers – and therefore that it can be a challenge to call God the Father, "Father."

But dear friend, given that we're trusting the Holy Spirit to transform us – *every* part of us – into the image of Jesus – can we not also trust Him to enable us to come to know our Father as Father?

It may indeed be difficult for some to utter that word; I understand from experience, having grown up with a father who was an alcoholic, and who was extremely abusive verbally to my mother and to me.

Nevertheless, the importance of knowing God our Father

as our Father (and we, His beloved, adopted sons and daughters, through Jesus) remains essential.

Here is an outstanding quote from author J.I. Packer that sums up the heart of this book; although long, it is *very much* worth a slow read, with careful consideration:

> *What is a Christian? The question can be answered in many ways but the richest answer I know is that a Christian is one who has God for his father...You sum up the whole of New Testament teaching in a single phrase, if you speak of it as a revelation of the Fatherhood of the holy Creator. In the same way, you sum up the whole of New Testament religion if you describe it as the knowledge of God as one's holy Father. If you want to judge how well a person understands Christianity, find out how much he makes of the thought of being God's child, and having God as his Father. If this is not the thought that prompts and controls his worship and prayers and his whole outlook on life, it means that he does not understand Christianity very well at all. For everything that Christ taught, everything that makes the New Testament new, and better than the Old, everything that is distinctively Christian...is summed up in the knowledge of the Fatherhood of God. "Father" is the Christian name for God.30*

**Beloved of God our Father, let me pray for you now:**

---

30 J.I. Packer, *Knowing God* (Downers Grove, Ill: InterVarsity Press, 1973), 181-182.

Father – Abba – I ask You now for my brothers and sisters in Christ that there would be a liberating, a transforming work that begins afresh in them this moment and for the remainder of their lives.

We ask You now, Holy Spirit, to help us to welcome You, to seek Your ongoing enablement to refer to our heavenly Father as Father, as Abba. We desire that You empower and free us to fully enter into our identity as sons and daughters of our Father.

Lord Jesus, in saving us and in showing us how to relate to the Father, You have set the example for us; You've shown us the way. Your crucifixion and resurrection was not merely for our salvation; that was only the starting point.

It was for our complete redemption – our eternal redemption. And we know from Your Word that we are sons and daughters of our Father because of Your work of redemption, Lord Jesus.

Strengthen us to daily "practice" the greatest spiritual delight – to call God our Father, "Father," or Abba. We ask this knowing it's Your will, in Your name and for Your glory, amen.

# DAY 29

## THE DEEP MEANING OF THE LORD (*YAHWEH*)

*For You are my rock and my fortress; for Your name's sake You will lead me and guide me. You will pull me out of the net which they have secretly laid for me, for You are my strength. Into Your hand I commit my spirit; You have ransomed me, O Lord, God of truth (Ps. 31:3-5)*

Because Yahweh is personal, active and faithful to keep covenant with us, we can learn to be content in whatever circumstances we find ourselves in. That is, He is in control of my life!

I *must believe* that God is in control of my life, even when circumstances don't align to my *perceived* favor, or when man *seems* to overlook me, or when I *feel* like I'm not getting "what I deserve."

It's in such situations that I must allow the truth and the power of God's Word to renew my mind, check my attitude, and lead me into humility before God. I must believe that even in adversity, He is leading and guiding me for His name's sake (v.3).

I must believe that if man seeks to do wrong to me, Yahweh – our Triune God -- will intervene (v.4). I must have the humility to "commit my spirit" to Him (v.5), knowing that I belong to Him, and that He alone has my best interests at heart.

However, if I believe I "deserve" this or that; if I carry a sense of entitlement, or that I'm better or more deserving than someone else who is in the place I want to be in, then I'm guilty of coveting; I'm guilty of pride.

It's then that I can be sure that God will resist me, because one of the promises in His Word (we love His positive promises, but tend to ignore the "negative" promises) is that He "resists the proud, but gives grace to the humble" (1 Pet. 5:5).

To operate in contentment brings God's peace, His favor, and His blessing – indeed, His presence! But to move in discontentment only grieves Him, and it results in the loss of His peace, His favor, and His presence.

It is truly a scary thing to choose to live in discontentment. But how grateful we must ever be to the Holy Spirit, who cares for our souls enough to bring that gentle, but firm conviction for us to repent of discontentment and draw near to Him in humility, thanking Him for what we have, and not for what we don't have!

Beloved, allow the Holy Spirit to search your heart now; ask Him to reveal any discontentment in you. If He does, repent of it, ask Him to forgive you and cleanse you, and to lead you into the vital exercise of declaring with gratitude all the things You can be thankful to Him for.

It's when we engage in this practice as a lifestyle that we learn to walk more deeply with our triune God, that we're truly free, and that we can experience the joy of the Holy Spirit.

# DAYS 30-31

## "HOLY" (*QADOSH*)

*In the year of King Uzziah's death I saw the Lord sitting on a throne, lofty and exalted, with the train of His robe filling the temple. ² Seraphim stood above Him, each having six wings: with two he covered his face, and with two he covered his feet, and with two he flew. ³ And one called out to another and said, "Holy, Holy, Holy, is the Lord of hosts, the whole earth is full of His glory" (Is. 6:1-3).*

Beloved, let us make it our life prayer to God to help us to see and understand that holiness is attractive; sin is disgusting; holiness brings God's life, His joy, and His peace; sin brings death, misery and destruction.

How have you thought of holiness? Have you thought of holiness as drudgery, as limiting, as restrictive, as a lifestyle of "do's and don'ts?

Given that "God is love" (1 John 4:8), and given all we've learned thus far about Him in this devotional, how can we possibly see His holiness as anything less a combination of His beauty, His purity, His love, His joy, His peace, etc.?

And yet, there is also something unique and awe-inspiring about holiness; Jerry Bridges writes of the three-fold description of God's holiness (Rev. 4:8):

God is infinitely glorious in all His attributes, but only His holiness is magnified with this threefold ascription. We never read that He is "wise, wise, wise" or "powerful, powerful, powerful," but twice we hear the heavenly throne attendants calling out "Holy, holy, holy is the LORD Almighty" (Is. 6:3; Rev. 4:8).[31]

Because this three-fold ascription came first in Isaiah, it's important for us to first consider the passage there (Is. 6:3), and the Hebrew word translated "holy."

E. J. Young, in his seminal three-volume commentary on Isaiah, informs us of God's holiness that "As here used, *qadosh* signifies the entirety of the divine perfection which separates God from his creation."

He correctly adds that God's holiness (*qadosh*) is His "unapproachableness…He is separate not merely from the creation but also from sin."[32]

Though obvious, it is paramount that we keep in mind that our two passages (Is. 6:3; Rev. 4:8) are set in the

---

31 Jerry Bridges, *The Joy of Fearing God* (Colorado Springs, CO: WaterBrook Press, 1998), 64.

32 Edward J. Young, *The Book of Isaiah*, vol. one, Chapters 1-18 (Grand Rapids: Eerdmans, 2000), 242 and footnote 19.

context of *praise*. Thus, Young again explains,

> To praise His name involves more than the mere repetition of the word *qadosh*. It includes deep meditation upon God and His attributes and the living of a life of humility in accordance with the precepts laid down in His Word. It is, in other words, the life of faith in Jesus Christ, lived for the glory of God.[33]

Can we *truly* appreciate God's holiness? Perhaps by understanding the historical background of the OT, we can at least gain a greater appreciation for His holiness, because of its utter uniqueness.

In his commentary on Isaiah, OT scholar John Oswalt points out to us,

> In the ancient Near East "holy" was not used especially widely, and when it was used, it was not given special prominence. It merely denoted that which sets deity, and that which belongs to deity, apart from the common. It had no moral connotations – and could not, given the variety of moral behaviors among the gods. But for the Hebrews, the idea of the holy was decidedly different. Beginning with Exodus 6:3 and continuing on through 19:6 and throughout the entire Old Testament, the word "holy" is given special prominence in describing Israel's God, occurring in all its forms more than eight hundred times.[34]

33 Ibid., 243.

34 Oswalt, *Isaiah*, 2575-2581 of 15434.

Alec Motyer also holds that *qadosh* primarily means "separateness," and is that "positive quality which distinguishes or defines God." Essentially, Motyer sums up what His holiness means when he argues that it is "his total and unique moral majesty."[35]

**Our God and Father – beautiful and majestic in holiness – there is *no one* like You! Help us to long to be like You in holiness (1 Pet. 1:13-19), so that we may know You as You are, so that we may prepare ourselves for our Lord's coming, and so that we may live with You for eternity.**

**Help us to daily remember that we live as aliens and strangers in this world, which is passing away – and also its lusts.**

**Help us to soberly, reverently believe and keep in mind that without holiness (sanctification), no one will see You (Heb. 12:14). Let us love Your holiness, walk in it, represent You before others by living holy lives.**

And may even this prayer bring You glory and honor, in Jesus' name, amen.

---

35 J. Alec Motyer, *The Prophecy of Isaiah: An Introduction and Commentary* (Downers Grove, IL: InterVarsity Press, 1993), 77.

# DAY 32

## HUMILITY (*PRAUTES*)

*"Come to Me, all who are weary and heavy-laden, and I will give you rest. Take My yoke upon you and learn from Me, for I am gentle and humble in heart, and you will find rest for your souls. For My yoke is easy, and My burden is light" (Mt. 11:28-30).*

To know our triune God is to know the One who – although He is omnipotent, omniscient and omnipresent – is also at His core, gentle, humble!

That is, He is not proud, arrogant, or egotistical. No wonder pride is an abomination to Him; no wonder He resists the proud – but gives grace to the gentle, the humble (1 Pet. 5:5-7)!

But what does this Greek word translated "gentle" (*prautes*) mean? *Prautes* is the humble and gentle attitude which expresses itself in a patient submissiveness to offense (recall 1 Pet. 2:19-23), free from malice and desire for revenge.

Didn't Jesus express this extraordinary characteristic as He submitted to the Father?

It's also the humility or meekness which is strength under control; it's the fruit of the Spirit which enables the believer to place the will of God before personal rights (cf. Gal. 5:23; James 3:13; Mt. 11:29; 5:5).

To be sure, Jesus lived this way before the Father as well. Therefore, beloved, when you and I seek to relate to and know the Lord Jesus, we ought to have in mind and in heart that He is gentle; He *is* approachable!

Likewise, we've already learned the great Hebrew word, noam (Ps. 27:4), which can be translated "beauty," "pleasant," or "delightful." Let us ask ourselves this question, then; when we think of God, do these descriptions immediately come to mind?

If they do not, why is that the case? And shouldn't we then desire to change that mindset which doesn't seem Him as He has revealed Himself to us?

Does He desire us to see Him as gentle, humble, beautiful, pleasant and delightful? How, then, may we know Him accordingly?

The answer is to ask! We can ask with confidence, knowing that these are things He's revealed to us in His Word (cf. 1 John 3:21-22; 5:14-15; Mt. 7:7-11).

**Our Father, we come into agreement with You and Your Word; Lord Jesus, thank You for revealing Yourself to us this way; knowing the truth of Your gentleness and humility, we also thank You that by coming to You so**

freely, we can have what You promise in Your Word (Mt. 11:28-30).

Holy Spirit, we now rely upon You to transform our minds and hearts to see You, our Father, and You, Lord Jesus as You really are. We ask these things in Your name, Lord; amen.

# DAYS 33-34:

## "THE LAW" (TORAH)

*How blessed is the man who does not walk in the counsel of the wicked, nor stand in the path of sinners, nor sit in the seat of scoffers! ² But his delight is in the law of the Lord, and in His law he meditates day and night. ³ He will be like a tree firmly planted by streams of water, Which yields its fruit in its season And its leaf does not wither; and in whatever he does, he prospers (Ps. 1:1-3)*

It's unfortunate and unhelpful that translators of the various English versions of Scripture translate Torah as "Law," in the sense that "Law" in no way conveys the richness of Torah.

Torah comes from the Hebrew verb *yarah*, which means to teach, or instruct. Thus, Torah means the "teaching" or the "instruction" of Yahweh. Given this, it's certainly no wonder that the psalmist exclaims, "Oh how I love Your Torah" (Ps. 119:97)!

None of this should surprise us, since Yahweh Himself

is called "Teacher" (e.g. Is. 30:20); He taught Moses (Ex. 4:15), and as part of His covenantal nature, He teaches His people (e.g. Ps. 25:12).

So great and gracious is He that He teaches sinners as well (Ps. 25:8). It is no mistake that both God the Son and God the Holy Spirit are called "Teacher" (cf. Luke 7:40; 11:45; 18:18; 19:39; 20:21, 28, 39; John 1:38, 49; 3:2; 8:4; 11:28; 13:13-14; 14:26; 15:22; 20:16; 1 Cor. 2:13).

Here is yet another aspect of the Triune God as One.

This is because the psalmist sees Yahweh as personally instructing him and the people of Israel, through His Word. Moreover, very little of the first five books of the OT – called the "Law" – is legal in nature; most of it is narrative!

The famed medieval Jewish rabbi Shlomo Yitzchaki (popularly known as Rashi) wryly, yet insightfully remarks,

> *If the Torah is essentially a book of law, why did God choose to start it with the stories of creation? Would it not have made more sense to begin with the first law commanded to the Jewish people?*[36]

Rashi's answer is brilliant; in quoting from Ps. 111:6, "He has made known to His people the power of His works, in giving them the heritage of the nations," Rashi explains that the Lord began His Torah with Creation to give the people of Israel a response to anyone who accuses

---

36 https://theisraelbible.com/reading-plan/genesis/

them of stealing the Land of Israel.[37]

Moreover, Rashi adds that since God is the creator of the world, it is His to give it to whomever he chooses. Though He initially gave it to the seven nations of Canaan, when they were no longer worthy, He chose to take it from them and give it to the Children of Israel.[38]

**Father, as the psalmist writes, I also declare to You: O how I love Your Torah! Your teaching, Your instruction refreshes me; it renews my mind; it produces the zeal I always need for You, and the love You enable me to have.**

**Today I ask that You always help me to hear Your Word – Your teaching and instruction – with hunger, ready obedience, and in faith.**

**Thank You, Holy Spirit for teaching me the way You do; I don't take this for granted, since it's one of a myriad of ways You enable me to fellowship with You.**

**Help me to glorify You by the way I carry out Your Word, in Jesus' name, amen.**

---

37 Ibid.

38 Ibid.

# DAY 35

## PEACE (*SHALOM*)

*"The steadfast of mind You will keep in perfect peace, because he trusts in You.* [4] *"Trust in the Lord forever, for in God the Lord, we have an everlasting Rock"* (Is. 26:3-4)

This word and its many derivatives is one of the most important and prominent in the OT and yet another extremely rich word (cf. Is. 26:3-4, where "perfect peace" is literally, "*shalom, shalom*").

*Shalom* appears approximately 250 times in the OT, in 213 separate verses. In 50-60 of those occurrences, it means "absence of strife" (e.g. 1 Kings 4:25).

It can mean "safety"; "wellness"; "wholeness"; "happiness"; "prosperity." It's that state of fulfillment which is the result of God's presence.

It can also mean completeness, harmony or fulfillment and "implicit in the idea of this word is the idea of unimpaired relationships with others and fulfillment in one's undertakings."[39]

To this day, Jews use the word for greeting and for saying goodbye and in fact, this is the case at least 25 times in the OT (e.g. Judges 19:20; 1 Sam. 25:6, 35).[40]

To wish someone *shalom* implied a blessing (2 Sam. 15:27), but to withhold *shalom* implies a curse (1 Kings 2:6).[41]

Beloved, what is the Holy Spirit asking you to do now, so that you can live in and to give out His *shalom*?

**Our Father, we find in the NT that by virtue of our relationship with Jesus, we already have peace with You through Him: "Therefore having been justified by faith, we have peace with God, through our Lord Jesus Christ" (Rom. 5:1).**

**However, though we have this peace positionally with You, we often lose it, and instead, we're bound by anxiety, strife, anger, bitterness, etc. The old hymn urges, "Trust and obey, for there's no other way, to be happy in Jesus than to trust and obey."**

**You want this for us; You've told us plainly in Is. 26:3-4. But we need Your help; please help us to never be ashamed to ask You for Your help, but also to immediately do what You call us to do, and that is**

---

39 Lloyd G. Carr, "shalom," in TWOT, vol. 2, 931.

40 Ibid.

41 Ibid.

to meditate on Your Word and then cast our burdens upon You. We ask these things in Jesus' name, amen.

# DAY 36

## "ANGER" (*AP*: PRONOUNCED "OFF"):

*"Sing praise to the Lord, you His godly ones, and give thanks to His holy name. ⁵ For His anger is but for a moment, His favor is for a lifetime; weeping may last for the night, but a shout of joy comes in the morning" (Ps. 30:4-5)*

In Ps. 30:5 (cf. also Ex. 34:6; Num. 14:18; Ps. 86:15; Neh. 9:17), we read that "His anger is but for a moment" (literally, in the blink of an eye). This word is the same word for "nose" or "face," and when used of God's anger, it involves an expression that we can visually understand.

In saying this, we must keep in mind that God is Spirit; He does not have a body. However, to communicate with us, He uses language and images we can relate to, in theology called an anthropomorphism.

The thought behind this word is that "God takes a long,

deep breath as he holds his anger in abeyance."[42]

Yahweh's anger is especially related to the sins of His people – particularly sins which are stubbornly held onto, with a refusal to repent. Indeed, such sinful attitudes "pains and deeply displeases him (2 Kings 13:3). Sin offends and wounds his love. The emotional response to this is divine anger."[43]

Let us carefully recall the remainder of Ps. 30:5, which is certainly an appeal to repent of sin from David, seen in the overall context of this psalm (and note throughout Ps. 32). In addition, it would be wise to examine Ex. 34:6; Num. 14:18; Ps. 86:15; Neh. 9:17, since these verses say so much to us about Yahweh's nature and character.

Just as human beings get angry over unjust, unrighteous and wicked acts, so does Yahweh. However, there is a major, even infinite distance between Him and us: we can only understand sin and justice partially; He understands it fully.

In his scholarly article on this Hebrew word, Gerard Van Groningen goes on to note, "This anger, though fierce (Jer. 25:37) is not sinful, evil, or the source of capricious attitudes or deeds. However, it is expressed in chastisement (Ps. 6:1; Is. 12:1) and punishment (2 Sam. 6:7; Jer. 44:4)."[44]

**Our Father, we've already learned from Ps. 27:4 that**

---

42 Gerard Van Groningen, "*ap*: Nostril, face, anger," in TWOT, vol. 1, 58.

43 Ibid.

44 Ibid.

You are pleasant; You're delightful. How we thank You from this study that these things have just been further reinforced for us!

# DAYS 37-38

## "MEDITATE" (*HAGAH*)

*"But his delight is in the law of the Lord, and in His law he meditates day and night" (Ps. 1:2)*

This word – usually translated "meditate," is especially noteworthy in Ps. 1:2 and Joshua 1:8.  A very broad word, its root refers to "inarticulate sounds," such as the growl of a lion over its prey (Is. 31:4), or of a groaning or moaning, in distress like a dove (e.g. Is. 38:14; 59:11).[45]

It can also mean to "sigh for," in sorrow or mourning; to moan for (Is. 16:7; Jer. 48:31). Closer to our idea of biblical meditation, it means to "utter" (e.g. Ps. 35:28; 37:36; 38:13; 71:24; Is. 59:3).[46]

But in Ps. 1:2; 63:7; 77:13; 143:5; Josh. 1:8 it very much

---

45 Francis Brown, BDBG, 211.

46 Ibid.

involves a speaking to one's self, by one's self and to one's self – as in a soliloquy – but it's in meditation.[47]

One Hebrew scholar is correct in writing, "Perhaps the Scripture was read half out loud in the process of meditation."[48]

A different, but frequent Hebrew word which also means to meditate is *siyach*: to muse (that is, to think about something carefully; to really think it through); to commune; to speak; to complain.

In effect, it is to go over a matter in one's mind, either inwardly or outwardly.[49] *Siyach* is used in 1 Chr. 16:9; Ps. 77:8; 9:12; 105:2; 119:15, 23, 27, 48, 78, 97, 148; 145:15.

Here are some examples of how I've learned to meditate on God's Word for 35 years, so far: **Thank You, Father for Your promise in Prov. 3:5-6, "Trust in Yahweh with all your heart and do not lean on your own understanding; in all your ways, know Him, and He will make your paths straight."**

As I'm declaring His Word, I'm seeing myself through the eye of faith leaning on Him, instead of my own understanding; I'm picturing myself not trying to figure the matter out.

I'm also seeing myself in faith opening my heart to Him and giving myself completely to Him. And I'm asking

---

47 Ibid.

48 Herbert Wolf, "haga," in TWOT, vol. 1, 467.

49 Gary G. Cohen, "siyach," in TWOT, vol. 2, 875.

Him and seeing myself being obedient to Him "in all my ways," and even simultaneously repenting for those areas of my life where I've sinned, or compromised.

Moreover, I think back to how He has indeed led and guided me in the center of His will throughout my life, as I've walked in these two verses.

Similarly, with Jer. 29:11-14, I've often said the first word, "I," many times – as if Yahweh Himself were saying this to me (which He is, through His Word).

I do the same with the word "know," and remind myself that He knows everything and I know nothing. I think of the word "plans" and remind myself of the plurality of the word, and let that build my faith.

Likewise, I continue to break down the rest of the verses, word-by-word. I did this just the other day with Rom. 8:28, and meditated on the words, "For we know" on a beach walk for probably a good 15 minutes.

As I did this, I asked myself if I really could include myself with what Paul said, but as I did, I let the words I spoke build my faith by declaring them.

Then I moved into the word "God," reminding myself that He is the object of my faith. I meditated on His sovereignty and providence in my life – from the "smallest" to the "greatest" areas I've needed Him.

When I came to the word "causes," I reminded myself (and the Holy Spirit reminded me) of this present-tense word and accordingly that God is active in my daily affairs.

Once again, I let the awesome power of His Word work in me and build my faith, thinking also of Heb. 11:6.

This is how I meditate on all of God's promises: "chewing" on His Word; talking to Him about His Word and in effect, letting His Word talk to me.

As the Hebrew words mean, I ponder their meaning and their power, their inspiration from the entire triune Godhead. I thank, praise, declare, pray and rejoice in the words from Scripture that I'm meditating on.

This is biblical meditation; there is nothing here that smacks of eastern meditation. On the contrary, even while meditating I'm revering God and His Word and still seeking to handle it accurately.

I want it to change me and transform me into the image of Jesus; that is the ultimate goal of the Word of God anyway.

This Word is so powerful that the devil does all he can to "snatch" it away from people who hear it. This is what Jesus teaches us in the Parable of the Sower (Mt. 13:1-23).

That Greek word translated "snatch" is the same word used of the rapture in 1 Thess. 4:13-18: It is a violent snatching up!

If Satan is that threatened by the power of the Word of God, shouldn't all believers conversely value it (by practicing it) with the same tenacity?

# DAY 39

## "GLORY" (*KABOD*; PRONOUNCED *KAVOD*):

*"Sing the glory of His name; make His praise glorious!" (Ps. 66:2)*

*Kabod* primarily refers to honor and its verb form means to be weighty, heavy, important or severe.

When referring to God's *kavod*, Scripture is telling us that He is more "important" than anyone or anything else; He is more "impressive" than anyone or anything else, and therefore, He is to be accorded with the highest "respect" than anyone or anything else.

This is the idea behind the two-fold use of this word, in Ps. 66:2: "Sing the glory of His name; make His praise glorious!"

When David calls us to "make His praise glorious," he is telling us (through the Holy Spirit) to worship Him intelligently, and from our hearts to know and declare His importance above all else, to revere Him above all else, and to be impressed with Him – above all else!

*Kavod* can also mean abundance or riches (Is. 61:6; 66:11-12). The root of this word and its derivatives appear 376 times in the OT, and its verbal use 114 times!

In terms of God's manifest glory (e.g. Ps. 145:5), there are 45 occurrences in the OT, usually accompanying the tabernacle, where He met with Israel (e.g. Ex. 16:10; 40:34) and with the temple (e.g. Ezek. 9:3).

God's *kavod* is inextricably linked with His holiness, since He is perfect and sinless and therefore without any defect whatsoever (cf. Num. 14:10; Is. 4:2; 6:3).

John Oswalt offers this important insight into kavod:

> **God's name is glorious in righteousness, faithfulness, judgment and salvation (Ps. 66:2; 79:9; Is. 40:5). He is the king of glory (Ps. 24:7-10), who has done gloriously. So he is not only to be honored because of his position as sovereign head of the universe, but because of his surpassing character in all realms.50**

Interestingly, God's glory is often described as "light" in Scripture (e.g. Ps. 19: 1-6; Is. 60:1-2; Ezek. 1:26-28; 10:4; 43:2; Mt. 17:2; Luke 2:8-9; 9:32; Rev. 21:23).

It surely is no coincidence that Jesus calls Himself "the light of the world" (John 8:12; cf. 1:4, 14; 9:5; 12:35), a

---

50 John N. Oswalt, "*kabed*," TWOT, vol. 1, 426-427.

clear claim to deity (cf. Rev. 1:16; Hab. 3:3-4).

**Our triune God -- Father, Son and Holy Spirit -- let everything within us give You the glory due Your name; You deserve the highest praise!**

# DAY 40

## "BLESS" (*BARACH*)

*"The Lord bless you, and keep you;* [25] *The Lord make His face shine on you, and be gracious to you;* [26] *The Lord lift up His countenance on you, and give you peace" (Num. 6:24-26)*

The Hebrew word to "bless" means to "endow one with the ability to succeed," and the context of the word will always determine its meaning.

Essentially, it is God's blessing upon man that enables him to succeed with God and with his fellow man, in every regard. Put another way, when God blesses a person, His favor and grace is upon that person.

So important is the word "bless" (*barach*) that God is ultimately its *only* source; *He* controls blessing and cursing (Num. 22), and it's only in His name that others can confer blessing (e.g. Deut. 10:8).[51]

---

51 Oswalt, "Bless," TWOT, vol. 1, 132.

As a result, those who are *wrongly* related to God can neither bless (Mal. 2:2), nor can they be blessed (Deut. 28) "and no efficacious word can alter this."[52]

However, the good news in all of this – so consistent with the NT – is that God desires to give His blessing to all who will trust Him (Gen. 12:3).[53]

Finally, when people "bless" God in the OT and NT, they're praising Him, or giving Him thanks for His own blessing to them.

Walter Kaiser rightly argues that the key to the *entire* OT – and one that undergirds the NT – is the idea of God's blessing upon humanity.

He writes, "It could also be seen as a divine plan in history which promised to bring a universal blessing through the agency of an unmerited, divine choice of a human offspring: 'In thee shall all families of the earth be blessed' (Gen. 12:3)."[54]

**Our Father, through Jesus Christ we're recipients of Your blessing, Your grace, and Your favor; please help us to never take these things for granted, but always to give You our full hearts!**

---

52 Ibid.

53 Ibid.

54 Walter C. Kaiser, *Toward an Old Testament Theology* (Grand Rapids: Academie Books, 1978), 13.

# DAY 41

## "LIFE" (*ZOE*)

*"I AM the way, the truth and the life (zoe); no one comes to the Father except through Me" (John 14:6)*

*Zoe* is a key word seen in John's gospel, appearing about 36 times in only 21 chapters. It's that unique quality of life resident in the Godhead alone, and which He exclusively shares with those who come to Him through faith in Jesus Christ.

This truth is powerfully seen in our quote above from John 14:6, as well as in John 17:3, where Jesus defines eternal life (zoe) as knowing both He and the Father.

The same can be said for John 3:16: "For God so loved the world, that He gave His only begotten Son, that whoever believes in Him shall not perish, but have eternal life (*zoe*)."

The opposite, however, should stir us with a great sense of

urgency to evangelism: "He who believes in the Son has eternal life; but he who does not obey the Son will not see life, but the wrath of God abides on him" (John 3:36).

In addition, consider Jesus' words in John 10:10: "But I have come to give you life (zoe), and that more abundantly."

*Zoe* is the sole reason and explanation for the qualitative difference between a believer who is genuinely walking with God and producing fruit for Him, and those who are "dead in their trespasses and sins" (Eph. 1:1-3).

Consider this as well, from John 1:4: "In Him was life, and the life was the Light of men."

**Our Father, this life You've given us through Jesus is the most costly and valuable life there is. May we be utterly humbled by Your free gift of eternal life! Likewise, may we be exceedingly grateful for this kind of life, and not take it for granted!**

**At the same time, help us to also recognize that we owe You everything; therefore, let us be zealous for You, for Your Word, and for obedience to You.**

**You deserve the highest praise from us, and You deserve the kind of lasting fruit that brings You glory and which serves as an example to believer and the unsaved. We ask these things confidently, knowing You desire to grant them, in Jesus' name, amen.**

# DAY 42

## "RENEW," "REFRESH," "REBUILD," "REPAIR" (*HADASH*)

*"He put a new (hadash) song in my mouth, a song of praise to our God; many will see and fear and will trust in the Lord" (Ps. 40:3)*

The "new" song (e.g. Ps. 33:3; 40:3; 96:1; 98:1; 144:9; 149:1; Is. 42:10) refers to the work of the Holy Spirit in us, which brings renewal or refreshing.

This rich word can also mean to rebuild, or to repair, and thus, the value and power of this word and what it can do in us through prayer, through praise and worship, and through God's Word.

Beloved, this is something we should *expect* from our Good Shepherd, especially since He's revealed this will of His in His Word! Truly, this comes from being in His presence through His Word, in prayer, or in praise and worship.

Yahweh promises to do a "new" thing for Judah, and those who love Him (Is. 43:18; 42:9; 48:6; cf. Jer. 31:22)

David uses this word to ask Yahweh to renew him after his sin (Ps. 51:10); Jeremiah asked Yahweh for the same thing (Lam. 5:21).

Regarding Yahweh's nature – seen in His *hesed* (plural) and in His compassion (*raham*; also in the plural) – Jeremiah said in Lam. 3:23 that these are "new" every morning (*hadash*).

Thus, He gives "new" life to the ground (Ps. 104:30), and He "renews" one's youth (Ps. 103:5).

Clearly, Yahweh is *the* source of renewal, refreshing, rebuilding and repairing – just as He is and does with His *zoe*!

**Oh, our *incredible* triune God! I want to thank You once again for Your idea of praise and worship. It has meant everything to me over the decades; You've used it powerfully in my life to increase my love, my devotion, my zeal, my prayer life!**

**Through praise and worship, You've drawn near to me so many times, surprising me with Your visitations, the way You speak to me to encourage me and build my faith!**

**I pray for all Your people now to enter into new dimensions in praise and worship; to be men, women and children who love praise and worship and to come to experience so much more from You.**

May You be glorified through this prayer, Lord Jesus, and may You teach us how to worship, Holy Spirit!

# DAY 43

## "FACE," OR "PRESENCE" (*PANEH; PANIYM*)

This morning I was asked a question via email about the meaning of the Hebrew word that is translated "face" (e.g. Ps. 51:11; 67:1). The question is an excellent one and it prompted me to do this word study for you, the reader.

In English, the singular is *paneh*; the plural is *paniym*. The root of this word is *pana*, which means to turn, in the context where God is expressing favor, pleasure, or delight in one of His own; it is to turn *toward* the person in blessing.

"Face" (which in Hebrew can also be translated "presence" or "countenance") is almost always in the plural in Hebrew because there are so many combinations of features of this rich word. The face identifies the person and reflects the attitude and sentiments of that person.

In the OT, "face" is often far more than a part of the

body; it reflects one who is engaged in behavior and is characterized by some personal quality.

Thus, one's "face" revealed a man's emotions, moods and dispositions. For example, a "hard" face was indicative of being defiant (Jer. 5:3), while a "shining" face reflected joy (Job 29:24).

A "shamed" face was evidence of defeat, frustration and humiliation (2 Sam. 19:5). An "evil" face is one that is marked by distress and anxiety.

A "fallen" face stems from very strong anger or displeasure (Gen. 4:5). So, for God to make His "face to shine upon us" (e.g. Ps. 67:1; Num. 6:24-26; cf. Ex. 33:14) involves His more than His countenance: it involves His presence, His favor, His blessing, His joy and His love.

Recall also how Jacob wrestled with God for His blessing, and after receiving it and realizing that it was God, called the place *Peniel* (Gen. 32:30), "for he said, 'I have seen God face to face, yet my life has been preserved.'"

The Hebrew word *liphne* is a preposition of the root *paneh* and means "before; in the presence of; in full view, under the eye of, at the disposal of, in the estimation of" (e.g. 1 Kings 17:1).[55]

This is the reason that I often pronounce the following benediction over the church at the end of a worship service:

---

55  Victor P. Hamilton, "panah," TWOT, vol. 2, 727-728.

*[22] Then the LORD spoke to Moses, saying, [23] "Speak to Aaron and to his sons, saying, 'Thus you shall bless the sons of Israel. You shall say to them: [24] The LORD bless you, and keep you; [25] The LORD make His face shine on you, and be gracious to you; [26] The LORD lift up His countenance on you, and give you peace (Num. 6:22-26)*

Our Father let us live in Your presence, and walk uprightly and blamelessly, so that we can "see" Your face (Mt. 5:8).

Please do make Your face to shine upon us, all the days of our lives; help us to be quick to seek Your face when You say, "seek My face."

And may the result of such time in Your presence be transformation in the lives of others. We ask these things in Jesus' name, amen.

# DAY 44

## "LOVE" (*AGAPE*)

*Love is patient, love is kind and is not jealous; love does not brag and is not arrogant, ⁵ does not act unbecomingly; it does not seek its own, is not provoked, does not take into account a wrong suffered, ⁶ does not rejoice in unrighteousness, but rejoices with the truth; ⁷ bears all things, believes all things, hopes all things, endures all things. ⁸ Love never fails (1 Cor. 13:4-8)*

What made Paul's constant use of *agape* special is that the society of NT times rarely used the word; Christians in fact took it over, since this word perfectly describes how God loved (and still loves) them (and us).

It also described how they ought to love one another. Leon Morris has a profound insight for us into the depth of meaning of *agape*:

> *Perhaps as good a way as any of grasping the new idea of love the Christians had is to contrast it with the idea conveyed by Eros...Eros has two principal*

*characteristics: it is a love of the worthy and it is a love that desires to possess. Agape is in contrast at both points: it is not a love of the worthy, and it is not a love that desires to possess. On the contrary, it is a love given quite irrespective of merit, and it is a love that seeks to give.*[56]

In addition, this love is a "caring love, a deliberate attitude of mind that concerns itself with the well-being of the one loved. self-devotion, not self-satisfaction, is its dominant trait."[57]

The best biblical definition we can find of agape can be seen in 1 Cor. 13:4-7; Paul's discussion there about agape provides a daily mirror for us, so that we can determine if we're walking in love toward others, or not.

**Father help us daily to choose to walk in this kind of love – *Your* love – with everyone.**

---

56 Leon Morris, *1 and 2 Thessalonians*, Tyndale New Testament Commentaries (Grand Rapids: Eerdmans, 2000), 43.

57 Curtis Vaughan, *Colossians,* The Expositor's Bible Commentary, vol. 11, ed. Frank E. Gaebelein (Grand Rapids: Zondervan, 1978), 218.

Made in the USA
Coppell, TX
16 April 2020

20138082R00074